MW00768686

Good Morning, Lowcountry!

Local knowledge, odd facts, recipes, survival tips for...

Living in the South Carolina swamp

Harriet McLeod

EVENING
POST
PUBLISHING
COMPANY
Charleston
South Carolina

EVENINGPOSTBOOKS
Our Accent is Southern!
www.EveningPostBooks.com

Published by
Evening Post Books
Charleston, South Carolina
www.EveningPostBooks.com

Editor: John M. Burbage
Design: Gill Guerry
Cover photos: Kendrick Mayes

First printing 2011
Printed in the United States of America

A CIP catalog record for this book has been applied
for from the Library of Congress.

ISBN: 978-0-9834457-9-1

Table Of Contents

"In that direction," the Cat said, waving its right paw round, "lives a Hatter. And in that direction," waving the other paw, "lives a March Hare. Visit either you like. They're both mad."

"But I don't want to go among mad people," Alice remarked.

"Oh, you can't help that," said the Cat. "We're all mad here. I'm mad. You're mad."

"How do you know I'm mad?" said Alice.

"You must be," said the Cat, "or you wouldn't have come here."

— Alice's Adventures in Wonderland

Acknowledgments

Thanks and appreciation to Pierre Manigault, chairman of the board, Evening Post Publishing Co.; and to John M. Burbage, president of Evening Post Ventures. Thanks and an oyster knife salute to Dan Conover, who coined the term "pluffmudder" and to Robert Behre, whose etiquette rules grace Chapter 7. Thanks, too, to the folks interviewed, quoted or referenced in this book. I am also deeply grateful to my family, great storytellers all, for their support. I'm especially grateful for my sister, Matey, and my brother, John, for their sense of humor and Lowcountry expertise.

Entrée

Parts of this book are based on my "Good Morning Lowcountry" columns that ran in the early part of the 21st century in The Post and Courier, the South's oldest daily newspaper, founded in1803. The rest is not-so-common knowledge. *Bin'yuhs* (see Chapter 8) have been around here long enough to know much of this stuff already, although they do forget. *Cum'yuhs* (ibid) will find this information vital to their survival in the heat, on the streets, among the gators and gnats, and at cocktail parties. People visiting from *Off* should first read Chapter 2 to find out what smells so, well, aromatic when the wind blows in off the marsh.

While pondering all this, remember to watch your step on Charleston's uneven blue slate sidewalks, Belgium block alleys, red brick roads and cobblestone streets, all of which have claimed ankles, elbows, teeth and self-esteem for the past few hundred years. As for finding your way through a maze of one-way streets in the charmingly redundant Old and Historic District, please know that everyone is polite but nobody can actually help you. If you ask directions, you could be stuck for 20 minutes listening to a *bin'yuh's* family history, restaurant recommendations and pothole-avoidance tips. Streets keep changing from one way to two ways and back to one way with the times, but they never get any wider. Bike lanes? Ha!

Also appreciate the fact that auto, bus, bicycle, golf cart, skateboard, horse carriage and cruise ship congestion here is not as bad as it's going to be. Charleston — which is at the heart of the Lowcountry — has always been notoriously slow. So don't worry about being late anywhere you go. Drawbridges, good gossip, and word that fresh shrimp are in at Shem Creek or Factory Creek or Jeremy Creek or Murrell's Inlet or that your crazy aunt is missing are perfectly acceptable excuses.

Note: Here in the Lowcountry, where eccentricity is prized, we citizens don't hide our crazy people in the attic. We put them right out there on the front porch where everybody can see them, and sometimes they do wander off. This little book is like that, too. So take your time and please enjoy!

Chapter 1:

You Can't Get There From Here

The Lowcountry is a collection of watery communities, most of them accessible by bridges, and Lowcountry people share the same view: flat from horizon to horizon, carpeted by miles of green marsh and domed with an unbroken sky that reflects its green and blue colors in the rivers and the ocean. The Lowcountry is also a state of mind, like Venice, another watery place that floods a lot, where the citizens consider themselves privileged. Therefore, borders are important.

After conducting extensive geological research to determine what comprises the South Carolina Lowcountry, then asking a few other *bin'yuhs* what they thought and finding everybody disagreed, the author made an executive decision:

The Lowcountry stretches along the S.C. coast from Murrell's Inlet in Georgetown County to the Georgia line near Savannah. It elbows inland toward Aiken, then northward along the sandy fall line past the lone Spanish moss-draped cypress tree that stands in the middle of the I-26 median near Bowman, and below lofty Manchester State Forest near Sumter almost to the badlands of North Carolina somewhere south of Dillon or thereabouts. NOTE: All of errant Horry County — which includes suctorial Myrtle Beach — is exempted for obvious reasons.

The Lowcountry's entire inland boundary has more to do with where the swamp ends than where the sand hills begin. Speaking of which, the Lowcountry has no hills, hence the name. It has a few sand dunes and some defensive earthworks made prior to two wars — both rebellions. Also above sea level are historic forts, American Indian shell middens (ancient trash piles, some 30 feet deep), church steeples and way too many gangly port cranes at Charleston.

The Lowcountry's greatest inclines are bridges, and because we live in such a watery place, distances are measured by how many of them you must cross to get there. Lowlands not already paved and covered with buildings are generally considered swampland, and our nearly year-round mosquitoes love it. Over the centuries, parts of the Lowcountry have been tamed while other parts continue to celebrate a beautifully unconstructed wildness. The tiny burg of Jamestown, for example, honors its own breeding grounds with the annual Hell Hole Swamp Festival.

The exceptional 1982 Wes Craven movie "Swamp Thing" was filmed in the Lowcountry, mostly *in* Magnolia Plantation and Gardens' Audubon Swamp about halfway up the Ashley River, three bridges from Charleston. The movie's grim interior scenes were filmed inside the historic Aiken-Rhett House in downtown Charleston. There, the film crew painted the parlor walls a hideous color that

Charlestonians dubbed "Swamp-Thing gray."

The movie is about a poor slob who is accidentally set on fire by a vicious villain, falls into the aforementioned bog and comes out a peculiar creature covered in pond algae and duckweed. "Science transformed him into a monster. Love changed him even more," explains the film poster, a collector's item around here. Good luck finding one.

Some of the Lowcountry's scarcer parts recall a "Far Side" cartoon featuring a man and a woman stuck in a car on the side of a road in the woods, with creeper vines and carnivorous plants crawling through the windows. The couple looks terrified, maybe by the thought that toothless rednecks with scraggly beards and chainsaws are somewhere close by. "I get the feeling we're not on I-95 anymore," the man observes.

Chapter 2

Questions a Tourist Might Ask

1) Why are porch ceilings painted light blue? What's that other blue color?

2) Why do the bricks look like that? What are those flat, black iron things on the bricks? What are those porch-like platforms with rails on rooftops overlooking the harbor?

3) What are grits?

4) Where was the red-light district way back when?

5) Where's the oldest bar in Charleston?

Bonus questions:

6) What's that smell?

7) Is it usually this hot?

1) The preferred Lowcountry porch ceiling color is robin's-egg blue. The somewhat brighter blue that trims windows and doors of small houses throughout the rural Lowcountry is "haint blue." Theories regarding the first include: It keeps birds from building nests in the corners and spiders can't stand it, therefore no webs to worry about. Facts regarding the second are: Since blue is the color of

heaven, paint your doors and windows with it and prevent *haints, hags, plat-eyes, wampus cats* and the like from slipping in and giving you a really bad case of indigestion.

Robert Russell, professor of architectural history at the College of Charleston, notes the color simply makes a porch feel cooler and is a purely emotional reaction. This makes good sense. When you're lying in a porch hammock, you're looking at sky blue — provided you're awake.

2) The most common brick pattern in 18th-century houses around here is Flemish bond, a header-brick/stretcher-brick, header-brick/stretcher-brick pattern, Russell says. Or you might notice a running bond, with the fourth or fifth brick starting a new series of header bricks. You will also see saw-tooth or dog-tooth cornices in 18th-century flat arches and 19th-century round ones.

The black iron medallions on the sides of older brick buildings are the end caps of what are called "earthquake bars." Lowcountry folks began sticking the rods through the walls of structures and bolting them tight to improve stability soon after the Great Earthquake of 1886, which knocked down just about everything from Ladson to Summerville to Charleston. The Great Quake of '86 killed more than 100 people and injured thousands.

Those balustrade-enclosed rooftop platforms are "widow's walks." Architect Sidney Stubbs notes that contrary to tradition, the decks were not used by worried potential widows watching for the return of seafaring husbands who were way too late for supper. He says they were lookout posts used by sharp businessmen searching the harbor for incoming shipping clients.

3) What are grits? Well, technically speaking, when whole kernels of corn are soaked in water and lye, you get softened germs called hominy. When hominy is coarsely ground, you get grits. When it's finely ground, you get cornmeal.

But according to "The Glory of Southern Cooking" and everybody else who knows anything about the subject, good hominy grits are made from crushed corn kernels neither de-germinated nor treated with lye. Rather, they are stone-ground to bits and sifted to remove the husks.

So-called Charleston bluebloods call it "hominy." Grits connoisseurs prefer the stone-ground kind over the bland, processed, quick-cook grits purveyed on grocery store shelves. For an intimate acquaintance with the latter, dress down for the spring World Grits Festival in St. George and actually roll in them. They have a contest that's sort of like mud rasslin' without the sex and violence.

4) Most of Charleston's earliest brothels were near the wharves on the east side of the peninsula in an area known as "Below the Drain" (more properly called South of Broad today). "Tradd Street, near East Bay, was pretty slimy until well into the 20th century. Most people forget that," Professor Russell notes. As shipping moved up the peninsula, houses of ill repute moved with it. Charleston was called the Holy City because its many tall church steeples marked the city silhouette seen from the water. But like any other colonial port, it was Sin City as well.

5) The oldest bar? Gable-roofed Coates' Row at 114-120 East Bay Street, just south of the Old Exchange Building, dates to the late 18th century. This structure, a liquor

store and high-end jewelry/watch shop now, was a tavern primarily for ship captains. It also had an extensive wine cellar, according to the late Burneston Baker, proprietor of the Tavern liquor store at 120 East Bay. Jonathan Poston writes in "The Buildings of Charleston: A Guide to the City's Architecture" that in the 1790s, Coates' Row was the meeting place of Charleston's Jacobin Club, a group largely made up of French immigrants who wholeheartedly embraced the spirit of the French Revolution.

6) Ah, the aroma! That distinctive smell which permeates the Lowcountry is the sea breeze, low tide, pluff mud, marsh gas, magnolias, Confederate jasmine, wisteria, gardenias, tea olive blossoms, carriage horses, storm drains, coffee grounds, shrimp hulls and kitchen smoke. The stench, on the other hand, is the paper mill to the north or the city's sewage treatment plant near the James Island Expressway.

7) Yes, it's usually this hot. But on late-summer days with a breeze, when small white cirrus clouds are inscribed across the pink-and-blue horizon like Chinese characters on an emperor's scroll, it's hard to mind.

Chapter 3

Pluff Mud: The Aroma of Primordial Ooze

A few years ago a *cum-yuh*, newly indoctrinated to the swamp, submitted these questions:

1. How do you pronounce *pluff,* as in "pluff mud"?
2. What exactly is pluff mud? I know it is marsh mud, but why a special name? Can this be compared to the Eskimos who have words for different types of snow? Does the Lowcountry need special names for the types of mud here?
3. Where did the name originate?
4. What does pluff mud smell like exactly?

Exhaustive research has resulted in the following answers:

1. *Pluff* rhymes with *fluff* and *puff.*

2. Pluff mud is one of the Eight Wonders of the Lowcountry — the others being the ACE Basin (Ashepoo, Combahee and Edisto rivers), Angel Oak, Charleston Harbor, Magnolia Cemetery, Fort Sumter, Charleston single

houses and the Coburg Cow. NOTE: The latter is a plastic, rotating bovine at the southwestern corner of Savannah Highway and Coburg Road, named for the popular dairy that used to be at the end of it on Wappoo Creek.

More specifically, pluff mud is the black, shoe-sucking, sticky stuff at the base of Lowcountry marshes. It has swallowed a sizable number of boaters' shoes, and is much easier to slide across on your stomach than to bog through. Pluff mud is the essence of the Lowcountry, the sweet-and-sour perfume of decaying crustaceans, dead amoebae, migrating duck droppings, Spartina grass, snail slime and salt water. For Lowcountry citizens, or *pluffmudders*, it's the smell of life.

Pluff mud was honored by the Winyah Bay Heritage Festival in Georgetown with bumper-stickers: "Pluff mud: The goo that holds the earth together."; "Pluff mud: It sucks the boots right off your feet!"; and "Pluff mud: You never forget your first time."

Scientifically speaking, "It's a very fine-grain mud largely composed of silt and other things that settle out in the marsh," notes David Whitaker, director of the Office of Fisheries Management at the S.C. Department of Natural Resources on James Island. "It has a fairly high organic level to it from decomposing plants."

Specifically, marsh mud is topsoil that runs off into rivers, which take it downstream and deposit it in mudflats. Lowcountry mudflats, writes Todd Ballantine, author of "Tideland Treasure: A Naturalist's Guide to the Beaches and Salt Marshes of Hilton Head Island," are a harsh habitat two to six feet deep.

Dying marsh grass releases nutrients that feed fish, shrimp, oysters and other saltwater creatures. But the mudflats are exposed at low tide. Fiddler crabs, snails, worms and other creepy life forms burrow into pluff mud's top layer, an anaerobic wasteland, to escape hot surface temperatures and predators. In this airless deposit of deceased gunk are oxymoronic microorganisms that live in the absence of oxygen. They putrefy marsh grass, thereby releasing hydrogen sulfide, which smells like rotten eggs that somebody on a dirt farm in Pelion forgot to gather during the last two weeks in August. That explains the smell.

Pluffmudders are not Eskimos. For one thing, our concept of a heavy snow is one that can be seen on top of a black car from *Off.* We have only one kind of residue here: pluff mud, although saltiness varies the farther inland you go. Pluff mud is special, though not unique to the Carolina Lowcountry.

"Georgia has it," Whitaker concedes. "They claim their pluff mud is darker and oozier than ours. We thought at some point we'd have a test to see whose is soupier." Any good grant writers out there?

3. Some pluffmudders say it's called pluff mud because *pluff* is the sound your car keys make after they fall out of your pocket and disappear into it. But it could be named for the 17th-century word *"pluff,"* defined by the Oxford English Dictionary as: 1. A strong puff or explosive emission of air, gas or smoke (as in the firing of gunpowder), or of dust; colloq., a shot of a musket or fowling piece. 2. To blow out smoke or air with explosive action, to puff; to discharge a gun, shoot.

Oxford cites the word's first use in 1663. Charles Town was founded in 1670 and musket fire was frequent in those days. Colonists might have heard the tiny, explosive puffs of hydrogen sulfide bubbling on the mud flat surface at low tide and were reminded of the *pluff* of "a fowling piece." Or would that be *ploof*?

Perversely, others who must not be from around here spell it PLOUGH and claim it derived from some weird pronunciation of "plough" or "plow." Pluff mud was plowed into Lowcountry cotton fields as a cheap, abundant fertilizer rich in peat at the doorstep of every Sea Island plantation, writes Theodore Rosengarten in "Tombee: Portrait of a Cotton Planter."

"Salt marshes are the most productive parts of the earth," he explains. "They sustain more organic matter per square foot and are capable of nourishing more herbivores by weight than any other soil. Marsh mud enriched the sandy cotton fields ... It made the cotton hearty."

4. Pluff mud smells like rotten eggs and old shrimp heads, or, from a broader perspective, like the funky, fecund soul of the primordial goo. You don't need a hot, wet late-summer day to smell it. You can appreciate it any time, especially at low tide.

Granted, other smells do interfere: Is that pluff mud or the paper plant? Is that horse manure or the city sewer system? Is that the tide turning or a hurricane coming? Natives and longtime Lowcountry citizens can differentiate these smells instantly. One is pheromonal, as in *eau de toilette*. The other is plain old *eau de* .... well, nobody really talks about that smell in public, but it emanates from the general direction of the carriage horse stables on Pinckney Street and the sewage treatment plant on Plum Island just across the Ashley River.

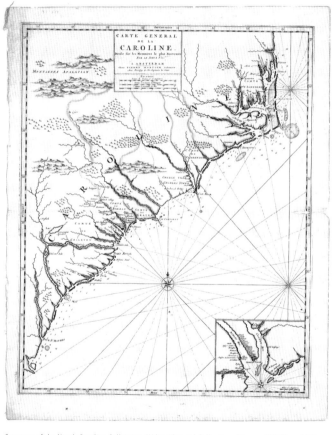

Courtesy of the North Carolina Collection, Wilson Special Collections Library, UNC-Chapel Hill

Chapter 4

Little State, Large Looney Bin

In 1860 distinguished Charleston attorney James L. Petigru criticized the signing of the Ordinance of Secession by observing to an acquaintance: "South Carolina is too small for a republic and too large for an insane asylum."

South Carolina's insistence that it had a Constitutional right to withdraw from the United States of America would be disastrous, Petigru had warned. But the state's firebrand leaders got their way. "The Union is Dissolved!" the Charleston Mercury headline declared on Dec. 20, 1860, and a second exclamation point was added on April 12, 1861 when Confederate Capt. George S. James at Fort Johnson on James Island ordered that a mortar shell be fired on Fort Sumter at the entrance to Charleston Harbor. The round exploded like a giant bottle rocket over the federally held fortress, and the four-year tragedy of the Civil War began.

It was an awesome sight, Charlestonians noted as they stood proudly on their rooftops in the charming old port city and watched the show. Most of them cheered. Only a few, like Mr. Petigru, understood the insanity of it all.

But today South Carolina again is lovely place, full of friendly people. Hence the hackneyed state slogan: "Smiling Faces. Beautiful Places," which is only slightly more detailed than South Dakota's "Great Faces. Great Places." Fact is, the Palmetto State's small, triangular locale in the southeastern region of the Lower 48 remains a large sanctuary for independent-minded fanatics.

From unreconstructed South Carolinians who didn't want to take the Confederate battle flag off the Statehouse dome nearly 150 years after what was left of the ragtag Rebel army stacked their arms and walked home; to Gov. Mark Sanford's taking a hike all the way to Buenos Aires to see his paramour, South Carolina continues to shine in the Straitjacket Hall of Fame.

The madness began in 1670 when Englishmen arrived at a point they named Albemarle not far up the Ashley River on the left bank. The construction of Charles Town proper began 10 years later downstream on Oyster Point at the tip of the peninsula where the Ashley and Cooper rivers converge, giving generations of tour guides the one-liner: "Charleston is where the Ashley and Cooper rivers come together to form the Atlantic Ocean."

Robert Rosen's "A Short History of Charleston" is a popular read around here for many reasons — one being it's short. Rosen points out that Charles Town got its early hedonist reputation by association with its namesake, the merry monarch King Charles II and his most convivial court. The early Lords Proprietors, who were granted Carolina in 1663 by happy-go-lucky King Chuck, supplied and sent over settlers, and made laws for the colony in hopes that their investments would soon pay off handsomely.

They were Anthony Ashley Cooper, Earl of Shaftesbury; George Monck, Duke of Albemarle; William Craven, Earl of Craven; Edward Hyde, Earl of Clarendon; John Berkeley, Baron of Stratton; Sir William Berkeley, brother of John; Sir George Carteret; and Sir John Colleton. Although their names are attached to towns, rivers and counties in the area, not one of them actually visited Carolina. They regarded the place, correctly, as pestilential.

Author and historian Dr. Nic Butler offers the following 12 little known or under-discussed facts of Colonial Lowcountry history:

1) It was an unhealthy place

The Lowcountry's history of pestilence is extraordinary. Yellow fever, typhoid, smallpox and venereal disease were common in the new colony. Malaria and dengue fever followed in the 19th century, along with cholera, *more* typhoid, pellagra, *more* smallpox, influenza, tuberculosis and *more* venereal disease.

According to the South Carolina Department of Health and Environmental Control's history of the region, epidemics of yellow fever, smallpox or both occurred in 1699, 1711, 1717, 1738, 1748, 1760 and 1799. The account is sprinkled with various efforts to control disease: the building in 1707 of a "Pest House" (for people *with* bugs) on Sullivan's Island; quarantines of offensive ships; investigations of privy vaults and cesspools; and ordinances against roaming dogs, goats and swine (since fences were not popular back then).

German traveler Johann David Schoepf, who visited Charleston in 1784, reports in his journal that Carolina was paradise in spring, hell in summer and a hospital in the fall. Charleston planters moved from their plantations to their town houses in May to escape heat, mosquitoes, gnats, biting flies, yellow fever, malaria and boredom. But what made Charles Town almost uninhabitable at first were typhoid and dysentery.

Letters back and forth between Lords Proprietors and those who received land grants said, "Look, this is an awful place. You need to move inland," Dr. Butler notes. "From 1680 to 1690, settlers were saying Charles Town is an unhealthy place, the water is bad, and it's no place for a proper town."

Rum helped solve the problem. With no sanitation systems, human and animal waste went directly into creeks, rivers and harbor. It also contaminated shallow wells. So a plentiful alcoholic distillate made from sugar was added consistently and in good measure to drinking water to kill those nasty bugs. They called it *punch*. It was the earliest water purification system. Unlike other "spirituous liquors," a license to serve it wasn't necessary.

2) Charleston, walled city

Charleston from the 1680s to the 1780s was a heavily fortified city, but soon after the Revolution was won, the wall came down and people forgot about it. A town gate was situated just north of the intersection of King and Calhoun (then called Boundary) streets.

"The city had walls and embrasures and platforms for the cannon and moats and drawbridges and brick columns and wooden gates with iron-strap hinges," Dr. Butler explains. "They knocked it down and built over it."

Why did the city need a medieval-type wall?

Charleston was settled on land occupied by Native

Americans but coveted by Spain and France. Pirates often called on the port as well. The wall was primarily an earthen structure on the land and brick along the waterfront. Approximately 2,700 feet of those bricks now lie under East Bay Street. Dr. Butler notes three places where the remnants of the original structure can be seen today:

— A portion of Half-Moon Battery, built between 1699 and 1701, is on display in the cellar of the Old Exchange Building at the east end of Broad Street.

— Not far south of the Old Exchange in the basement of the Missroon House, 40 East Bay Street, is what's left of the Granville Bastion.

— To the north, on the green in Marion Square, a section of a tabby wall has been preserved. It is part of the late-colonial Horn Work Battery.

3) Garbage

Much of the peninsula is landfill. As early as the 1690s, a licensed scavenger stopped in front of houses and rang a bell, notifying residents it was time to bring out the garbage. These scavengers were salaried white men who used slaves for most of the dirty work. The garbage was gleaned of anything of value and dumped in the peninsula's plentiful salt marsh to create high ground. Generally speaking, this system continued until the early 1960s when it dawned on folks that the marshes are critical for maintaining a healthy environment and didn't deserve to be treated that way. Today's city police headquarters and municipal courts on Lockwood Boulevard are built atop one of the old garbage dumps. So is Brittlebank Park, just across the street on the Ashley River.

4) Urban slaves

So-called "nominal slaves" lived somewhat independently around town, worked various jobs as assigned by their legal owners and were allowed to keep a portion of the pay. As early as the 1690s, Colonial legislators complained about this practice because it sanctioned competition with white craftsmen. In 1750 a law was passed requiring that slaves who worked on such a lease arrangement be issued badges. These so-called "slave badges" were an identification system and a mostly urban phenomenon.

Those who wore them worked as porters, carters, draymen, carpenters, masons and blacksmiths. There were considered "idle slaves" whose expertise was needed on a relatively short-term basis. The owner of an enslaved master mason, for example, could lease him out for months until the job was done. As long as the craftsman carried his identification badge, he was fairly safe to come and go around town without being hassled by ever-watchful authorities.

5) Attack of 1706

Charleston repelled a combined attack by the Spanish, the French and their American Indian allies in 1706, thanks to residents using the "homeland security" approach. They organized a militia, built walls around the city, stockpiled gunpowder, spread the word that they had a great network of spies in the hinterlands, prepared fully to defend themselves and hoped it would all work out. When the invaders sailed into the harbor in 1706, they surveyed the scene and said, "Oh, crap, they've got a wall," then tried to land on James Island instead. The local militia had units stationed over there and chased them off, so the invasion force landed near Hobcaw, east of the Cooper

River, instead. But the militia chased them off again — all the way up to Bull's Bay near McClellanville where the invaders decided it would be best to pack up and go home.

6) Slaughterhouses and markets

Charleston slaughterhouses were located close to creeks on the upper east and west sides of the peninsula. The creeks were important because animal carcasses and offal could be carried off with the tides. High priests of these abattoirs dispatched hogs, cows, goats and sheep, then carted the meat downtown to sell at the market. Interestingly, Ashley Hall — Charleston's all-girls preparatory school on the west side — is in the heart of an area once known as Butcher Town. A nearby millpond was the repository of blood and guts left over from the slaughter. The pond was filled with garbage and covered with dirt in the 1850s.

"Early markets were on the waterfront, and bunches of common people and slaves congregated there every day. There was a beef market at City Hall (at Broad and Meeting streets). Vegetables and meat were on the east end of Tradd Street. Water Street until 1790 was a parking lot for canoes. We forget that today. By the early 19th century, they were calling them farmers' markets," Dr. Butler says.

7) Cattle hunters

America's first cowboys were mostly slaves. Before rice, and long before cotton, a major business of the colony was exporting beef to the Caribbean. The animals were slaughtered and the meat cured, packed in barrels and shipped to Barbados. The cattle would free-range the woods during winter, then be rounded up and driven in from areas as far away as Cainhoy and Goose Creek to the slaughterhouses just north of town. Legislation was passed stipulating that at least one white man be included among the enslaved drivers.

8) Windmills

Producing energy using wind power is not new in the Lowcountry. Dutch settlers might have been responsible for building the first windmills here in the 1700s. One was set up at White Point Garden early on, and another was erected on the point of Fort Johnson on James Island in 1708. An 1802 map shows three windmills used at lumber mills on the banks of the Ashley River.

9) Driving on the left side of the road

South Carolina was a British colony therefore horse-drawn carriages were driven on the left side of roads and streets. Rules of the St. Cecilia Society, Charleston's exclusive musical and dance society formed in 1766, included specific instructions when traveling to an orchestral performance or ball. To wit, when the society was housed on the northwest corner of Bedon's Alley in 1787, it tried to prevent traffic congestion by announcing: "It is entreated that carriages will put down with their horses heads toward the bay, and take up with their heads to Church-street." It wasn't until 1849 that the city council passed a law that set things "right" — as they are today.

10) Powder explosion of 1780

There were at least four powder magazines in colonial Charleston. The one that remains is on Cumberland Street and is a tourist attraction today. It was taken out of actual munitions service, visitors will be relieved to know, in 1746.

Anyway, on May 25, 1780, days after the British recaptured Charleston, soldiers stacked confiscated weapons in a powder magazine, or a storage facility appropriated for that purpose, near Archdale Street. Something sparked an explosion that killed more than 200 people.

"It killed everybody within a few hundred feet," Dr. Butler says. "The magazine was full of powder and muskets. It was raining ramrods and bayonets. Body parts were flying. Eyewitness descriptions said burnt people were writhing like worms on the ground. There were descriptions of people without arms and legs. William Gilmore Simms (later) claimed that after the blast, the Second Congregational Church, now the Unitarian Church, was splattered with blood."

11) Slave musicians

Slave musicians accompanied their masters' militia muster and performed in parades before the Revolutionary War. Plantations often had a resident slave fiddler and others received formal musical training. In antebellum days, it was popular for a young man to hire a slave band to help him woo his sweetheart. Slave musicians also performed for white social gatherings and black celebrations. "Slave dances were illegal but they happened," Dr. Butler says.

Black instrumentalists of the 19th century held a special position in the South's rural black community, Paul A. Cimbala, professor of history at Fordham University, writes in "The Journal of Negro History." They brought slaves together for a "frolic," one of their few group social occasions. Their neighbors called them "musicianers." "Musicianers" was also the term used to describe Irish-American musicians in urban Charleston in the 1870s, Dr. Butler says.

12) Horse racing

The Lowcountry was no stranger to the sport of kings. The first races were held in 1734 north of Charleston in St. James Parish-Goose Creek. In 1735 the York Course was laid out closer to town, on the Charleston Neck at the junction of Old Dorchester Road and what is now Meeting Street Road. Annual meets and races were held at the York Course until 1760, when the New Market Course opened east of the city's Broad Path (King Street). Races were an annual event until they were interrupted by the Revolutionary War; they resumed after the war and continued until 1791.

The South Carolina Jockey Club, first formed in 1734, was reorganized by a group of gentlemen in 1758. The Lowcountry's golden age of racing began in 1786 when some 20 planters and breeders laid out the Washington Race Course (present-day Hampton Park). Race Week, held at the course each February, became the highlight of Charleston's winter social season. Horse breeders were from South Carolina's most prominent families, including the Alstons, Middletons, Stoneys, McPhersons, Sinklers and Singletons.

In 1747 Edward Fenwick built a stud farm and three-mile racetrack on the Johns Island plantation he had inherited and began importing Thoroughbreds from England. Among the studs he brought to Fenwick Hall was Brutus, an offspring of the famous Matchem, which came from the breed's original Godolphin Arabian stud. Brutus was famously successful in South Carolina horse racing and as Fenwick's home stud.

Chapter 5

You Say Geechee, We Say Gullah

"Gullah" is the name given to descendants of enslaved West Africans brought to coastal South Carolina starting almost 400 years ago. Dr. Lorenzo Turner, in his seminal study of Gullah language in 1949, attributed the name to the Gola tribe along the Sierra Leone-Liberia border.

In Georgia, the culture is called Geechee. Dr. Turner traced "Geechee" to "Gidzi" (pronounced geezee), which is the word Africa's Mende tribe used to describe people in the border region of Sierra Leone, Liberia and Guinea.

Some black South Carolinians prefer the term Geechee to Gullah; others like neither. While Gullah has been researched and documented as a language spoken by the descendants of West African slaves, "Geechee" has, at times, also been used to describe the distinctive accent of white Charlestonians. Adding to the confusion is Georgia's beautiful Ogeechee River, which empties into Ossabaw Sound south of Savannah. Its name is of American Indian origin. Georgia's Geechee people, many of whom live in the once isolated Ogeechee River basin and on Georgia's nearby barrier islands, may be named for the river.

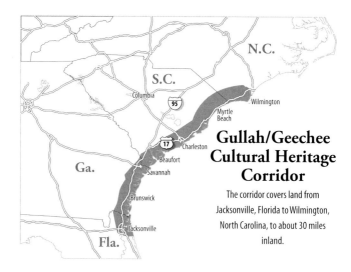

**Gullah/Geechee
Cultural Heritage
Corridor**

The corridor covers land from
Jacksonville, Florida to Wilmington,
North Carolina, to about 30 miles
inland.

Regardless of terminology, the Gullah/Geechee Coast
and culture are considered by the National Trust for Historic Preservation to be one of the most threatened historic
areas in the United States. Rapid coastal development has
led to the loss of long-held African-American family land
and traditions.

In 2005, Congress passed legislation introduced by
Congressman James Clyburn of South Carolina that cre-
ates a Gullah/Geechee Heritage Corridor, the coastal re-
gion that stretches from 30 miles inland of the Cape Fear
River in North Carolina south to the St. Johns River in
Florida. Public hearings were held in 2009 in towns, cit-
ies and communities along the corridor including Mount
Pleasant, McClellanville, Johns Island, Hollywood; Wal-
terboro; Yemassee; St. Helena Island; Beaufort; Bluffton;
Hardeeville; Pinpoint, Ga.; Darien, Ga.; Savannah, Ga.;
St. Simons and Sapelo islands, Ga.; Wilmington, N.C.;

Jacksonville, Fla.; and Fernandina Beach, Fla.

"In the past, Gullah culture was considered, by some members of the culture, something not to be proud of," says author and journalist Herb Frazier of Charleston. "But I think people can draw a sense of pride just that there is a corridor designation. Black people around the country, because of our ancestry, share a sense of family. This culture primarily in South Carolina and Georgia is connected to people all over the country along traditional patterns of migration. The continuity and preservation of Gullah culture depends on the retention of property, families living close together and living off the land. A lot of Gullah speech is no longer spoken like it was in the 1930s. Gullah people have always lived close. If you lose the land, you lose the culture."

Michael Allen, National Park Service coordinator for the Gullah/Geechee Heritage Corridor, agrees.

"I see Gullah/Geechee culture as a foundation of the development of our American journey. It's now being recognized as the gift it is here in the 21st century. As I travel up and down the corridor today, I encounter the people from three centuries ago in their descendants' voices and inflections, in their art and crafts, in their kitchens, in their marriage ceremonies, in their places of worship. Gullah/Geechee culture in America probably has the highest level of retention of Africanisms. Because of that retention, there's uniqueness, and there's an awareness of its genesis on the other side of the Atlantic."

"De Fox en De Crow"

The Gullah storytelling tradition goes back to the griots of Africa. Storytelling is only one of the customs passed down from African ancestors that survive today and include religious practices, cuisine and the making of baskets similar to those woven in Sierra Leone. For the flavor of the language, here's a sample from the Gullah retelling of an Aesop fable recorded by author Ambrose Gonzales in 1923 and translated by historian Joseph Opala, who teaches at James Madison University. "De Fox en de Crow" is about a trickster fox trying to talk a crow into dropping the piece of meat she has in her beak.

Gullah:

Den, Fox staat fuh talk. E say to eself, a say, "Dish yuh Crow duh ooman, enty? Ef a kin suade um fuh talk, him haffuh op'n e mout, enty? En ef e op'n e mout, enty de meat fuh drop out?"

Fox call to de Crow: "Mawnin tittuh," e say. "Uh so glad you tief da meat fum de buckruh, cause him bin fuh trow-um-way pan de dog ... E mek me bex fuh see man do shishuh ting lukkuh dat."

Crow nebbuh crack a teet! All-time Fox duh talk, Crow mout shet tight pan de meat, en a yez cock fuh lissin.

English:

Then, Fox started to talk. He said to himself, he said, "This here Crow is a woman, not so? If I can persuade her to talk, she has to open her mouth, not so? And if she opens her mouth, isn't it true the meat will drop out?"

Fox called to the Crow: "Morning girl," he said. "I am so glad you stole that meat from the white man, because he would have thrown it away to the dog ... It makes me vexed to see a man do such a thing as that."

Crow never cracked open her teeth! All the time Fox was talking, Crow's mouth was shut tight on the meat, and her ears were cocked to listen.

Chapter 6

How to Eat an Oyster

Lowcountry cuisine is a hefty combination of edibles from land and sea, spiced with African and Caribbean influences and often sweetened just right with pure cane sugar. To better understand the menus of some of the Lowcountry's authentic home-cooking restaurants, it's important to know that locals typically choose from their five favorite food groups — sugar, salt, biscuits, shrimp and oysters; and from four subgroups — grease, hush puppies, fish, crabs and alcohol. Of these, oysters are the favorite. They sometimes disgust people from *Off*, but nobody around here really cares.

The succulent bivalves have been around for 65 million years and have been a staple of the Lowcountry diet for at least the last 4,000 of them. As the saying goes, the first person to eat an oyster was unusually brave, a common trait of pluffmudders. Besides, if God didn't intend for us to eat oysters, he wouldn't have stuck them in tidal creeks where they can be picked up, taken to shore, removed from their shells and swallowed raw (preferably chilled on ice), steamed, fried and stuffed in turkeys at Thanksgiving. Eating fresh oysters is one of the Lowcountry's oldest traditions.

Shell middens (a fancy word in England for "dunghill" but locally for "trash heap") are scattered throughout South Carolina's coastal marshes. There's one on Fig Island, a National Historic Landmark near Wadmalaw Island; another is off U.S. Highway 17 North at the eastern edge of the Francis Marion Forest.

Indigenous pluffmudders paddled down from the mountains during summer and fall for centuries to their campsites along the coast, gorged themselves on oysters, conchs, mussels and clams, and tossed the shells in what became monumental piles.

The Indians eventually built walls on top of these ever-growing shell piles for shelter and defense. They also dug pits atop the mounds in which they built fires so they could steam fresh seafood and roast venison and other meats. Some constructed "rooms" with palm-frond roofs at the sites. Most of these creekside campsites have been looted, leveled or covered with dirt through the years. One of the latter is a tall grassy hill overlooking the Ashley River on The Citadel campus, near the mess hall.

So, how do you cook and eat an oyster? The best route between and an oyster and your mouth is a Lowcountry oyster roast.

First, spray the oysters with water using a garden hose to knock off the mud. Then dig a pit and build a fire in the bottom. Cover the pit with a wide sheet of sturdy metal. Shovel oysters on top of this "grill" and cover them with wet burlap. Don't roast them too long; the juicier the better. Shovel them from the grill onto a wooden table with a hole in the middle of it. Under the hole, place a bucket for the empty shells. Put an oyster glove on one hand, and grab an oyster knife with the other. Pick up a cluster of hot oysters and place it on the table in front of you. Don't cut yourself. Put your knife tip at an oyster's hinge, the narrowest point. Dig and pry. Dig and pry some more. (It takes some doing.)

When you get it open, cut the muscle that holds the oyster to its shell. Pick up the oyster with the flat blade of your knife and your thumb. Dip it in butter or ketchup mixed with horseradish, if you like. Tilt your head back and drop it in your mouth. Try not to think about the texture of the slippery suckers or you might gag. SIDE DISH: Saltine crackers.

A few more Lowcountry delicacies:

Ben Moise's Frogmore Stew

A Lowcountry Boil can be junked up with anything from onions to chicken breasts, but then it's not Frogmore Stew, named for the community of Frogmore on St. Helena Island in Beaufort County. (Don't go looking for Frogmore, by the way. Its post office has been renamed St. Helena and the old road signs have been changed.)

Traditional Frogmore Stew has only smoked sausage, ear corn and shrimp in it. Don't add potatoes to the pot, says Ben Moise, retired game warden, author and sometime caterer who makes the stew by the vat-full. The starch in the potatoes makes the shrimp too slippery to peel. "I have been doing the doggone thing for close to 30 years," he says.

6-8 ounces of unpeeled shrimp per person
1½ ears of corn per person
5 ounces of Hillshire kielbasa per person

Use a big pot that holds roughly twice the volume of water as the volume of the ingredients. A container with one of those perforated inserts for easy draining is preferred. Put a good double handful of Old Bay Seasoning into the water. Boil the sausage and the corn for 12 minutes. Add the shrimp or cook the shrimp separately for 2 to 2½ minutes. "Once we drain 'em, we dust 'em again with Old Bay," Moise says. "It's a perfectly rustic, elementary dish."

Margaret McLeod's Shrimp Creole

¾ cup sliced onions
1 cup coarsely chopped celery
4 tablespoons butter
3 tablespoons flour
1 teaspoon salt
1 tablespoon chili powder
1 cup water
2 cups canned tomatoes
1 tablespoon vinegar
1 teaspoon sugar
2 cups boiled, peeled shrimp

Sauté the onions and celery in the butter. Add flour, salt, chili powder and water (a little at a time) to make a *roux*. Simmer for 5 minutes. Add canned tomatoes, vinegar, sugar and, just before serving, the peeled cooked shrimp. Serve over hot rice. Serves 4.

Hoppin' John

Although we're lucky just to be here, good fortune in the Lowcountry is *guaranteed* on New Year's Day by eating Hoppin' John and collard greens. The greens are the vegetable equivalent of a seven-day "Pay Me Now" candle, a quick-cash magical entreaty that used to be sold in local drugstores. Candle burning was part of the folk rituals — including incantations, spells and herbal potions — performed by African-American spiritual root doctors in the South.

Hoppin' John is most effective when made with field peas. Elsewhere, they might use black-eyed peas, but Charlestonians, particularly and, of course, peculiarly, are adamant about the field peas. The name Hoppin' John comes from a Creole and Gullah corruption of *pois a pigeon*, pronounced "pwa peezhawn," the rice-and-pigeon-peas dish of France and the Caribbean. Say "pwa pee zhawn" a few times fast at it begins to sound like Hoppin' John. This recipe is from cookbook author Nathalie Dupree, with hog jowl added.

2 cups dried field peas, soaked overnight and drained
A slice of hog jowl
1 jalapeno or other hot green pepper, chopped
1 red onion, chopped
½ cup celery, chopped (about 2 ribs)
Salt
Freshly ground black pepper
8 cups chicken stock
1 cup uncooked rice
3 green onions or scallions, chopped
3 slices bacon, fried, drained on paper towels, crumbled

Place the peas, hog jowl, hot pepper, red onion, celery, and salt and pepper to taste into a large pot. Cover with the chicken stock. Bring to a boil, reduce the heat and cover. Simmer until the peas are tender, about 1½ to 2 hours. Add additional water as needed. Drain the peas, reserving the liquid. Discard the hog jowl. With the reserved liquid (about 3 cups), cook the rice in a small pot, covered, until the liquid is absorbed and the rice is tender, about 20 to 25 minutes. Fluff with a fork. Mix together the peas and rice. Place in a large serving bowl. Sprinkle with the chopped green onion and crumbled bacon if desired.

Mepkin Abbey Cinnamon Buns

The late Brother Boniface Schnitzbauer, monk of Mepkin Abbey, the Trappist monastery in Berkeley County, was master of the Mepkin kitchen for 40-plus years and a superb baker. The late Abbot Francis Kline told visitors Brother Boniface considered baking "an art and a very sacred duty." Schnitzbauer published his first cookbook, "Baking with Brother Boniface," at age 90. Mepkin Abbey, by the way, no longer sells eggs, thanks to a run-in with PETA. Now they're growing "the world's first Trappist mushrooms." Find them at Piggly Wiggly grocery stores.

Dough:
2 packages active dry yeast
½ cup warm water
2 teaspoons sugar
1 cup milk
¼ cup butter, melted
¼ cup sugar
2 eggs

5 cups bread flour
1 teaspoon salt

Filling:
¼ pound butter, melted
Cinnamon sugar (½ cup sugar mixed with 1½ teaspoons ground cinnamon)
2 cups raisins, soaked and drained
Egg wash (1 egg beaten with 1 tablespoon water)

Glaze:
1 cup confectioners sugar
1 to 2 tablespoons (or more) boiling water
1 teaspoon lemon juice

Preheat oven to 350 degrees. Dissolve yeast in ½ cup warm water with 2 teaspoons sugar and set aside for 10 minutes until mixture starts to bubble. Gently heat milk, butter and ¼ cup sugar in saucepan. Cool. Whip eggs into milk mixture. Measure flour and salt into a bowl. Make a well in the flour. Add milk mixture and yeast mixture into the well. Blend flour in with a fork until all ingredients are well-mixed. The dough will be sticky.

Place dough on a work surface that has been lightly dusted with flour. Work dough with your hands until dough no longer sticks to your hands. Don't add more flour unless necessary. Place dough in a greased bowl. Keep in a warm place and let rise until doubled. Roll dough into a rectangular shape ¼ inch thick. Brush with melted butter and sprinkle with raisins and cinnamon sugar. Roll lengthwise and cut roll into 14 slices. Place buns, cut side down, into two greased 9-inch round cake pans. Let rise in pan until doubled. Brush with egg wash. Bake at 350 degrees for 30-35 minutes, or until golden brown. While buns are still hot, sprinkle with remaining cinnamon sugar and drizzle with glaze. Makes 14 buns.

Benne Seed Wafers

The West African slave trade introduced sesame seeds to America, along with okra, yams, black-eyed peas, peanuts and the banjo. The Mende tribe's name for sesame seeds, "benne," stuck in the Lowcountry where Gullah people maintained the language and traditions of their forebears. Benne seed wafers are a Charleston classic.

Find instructions for Benne Seed Wafers, Benne Cookies and Very Thin Benne Cookies on pages 267 and 268 of "Charleston Receipts." Or, if you don't want to look it up …

¾ cup butter
1½ cups brown sugar
2 eggs
¼ teaspoon baking powder
1¼ cups flour
½ cup toasted benne seeds
1 teaspoon vanilla

Cream butter and sugar together and mix with other ingredients, in the order given. Drop with a teaspoon on waxed paper in pan far enough apart to allow spreading. Bake at 325 degrees until brown. TIP: When you take the pan out of the oven, slam it down on the counter to flatten out the benne cookies.

N'Awlins Iced Coffee

New Orleans is a city that, like Charleston, wears humidity like a wet dog. The Lowcountry prefers iced tea, sweet or unsweet, with or without lemon, but constantly and in big glasses. Sharing this word-of-mouth recipe for iced coffee from the City That Care Forgot down on the Mississippi River seemed like a good idea. Lowcountry citizens can always use more caffeine, especially if we can get an afternoon nap later.

Get a pound of ground coffee. Any kind will do, but coffee with chicory is good. Dump it into a sun tea jar, or any gallon jar. Fill the jar up to its brim with COLD water from the tap. Stir the grounds down. Add a tablespoon, or two, of vanilla. Stir the grounds again before you put the lid on. Let the jar sit overnight. The next day, lift off the grounds at the top and throw them in the garden. Strain the rest of the coffee through a filter, a little bit at a time, into another jar. You'll be left with heavy, dark coffee liquor. Pour two or three fingers of coffee liquor over ice and fill to the top with cold milk. Add sugar as you like. Stir it up.

Eating tips for the holidays:

1. Do not have a snack before going to a party. The whole point of going to a party is to eat other people's food for free. Same goes for beer, wine or liquor.

2. If you see carrot sticks, leave. Go next door where they're serving bourbon balls.

3. If you come across something like barbecued shrimp, station yourself near them and eat as many as you can before annoying other guests.

4. Drink eggnog. Who cares if it has 10,000 calories?

5. Under no circumstances should you exercise during the holidays. You can do that in January when you have nothing else to do but pay bills. This is the time to take a nap, which you'll need after circling the buffet table with that 10-pound plate of food.

6. Mashed potatoes should be made with whole milk, if not heavy cream.

7. If something comes with gravy, pour it on.

8. Eat pie *and* cake. What other time of year do you get to have more than one dessert?

9. Fruitcake is loaded with the mandatory celebratory calories, but ignore it. Fruitcakes make good bookends.

10. If you don't feel terrible when you leave a party, you haven't been paying attention. Reread the tips.

Chapter 7

Etiquette: Well, Bless Their Hearts

For 11 consecutive years, Marjabelle Young Stewart, known as the Queen of Couth, awarded Charleston the title of Most Mannerly City in America. Charleston retired with the championship belt and, maybe because its domination of the field was becoming embarrassing, places like New York and Savannah began to win the award.

Charleston's modern manners are informed by a historical imperative. In his journal, "Travels in the Confederation 1783-1784," German writer Johann David Schoepf remarks:

"The manners of the inhabitants of Charleston are as different from those of the other North American cities as are the products of their soil ... Throughout, there prevails here a finer manner of life, and on the whole there are more evidences of courtesy than in the northern cities ... On the way hither, the farther I traveled from Pennsylvania towards the southern country, there were to be observed somewhat more pleasing manners among the people. At least there was absent the unbearable curiosity of the common sort, which in the more northern regions extends to shamelessness and exhausts all patience. There is courtesy here, without punctiliousness, stiffness or formality."

In the Lowcountry, we smother people with hospitality. We ask questions of visitors to show our interest in them. If they ask questions of us, we take the opportunity to tell them the names of our dogs. We don't talk about money, religion or politics to people we don't know well, and sometimes not even to those we do.

These etiquette rules are not as exhaustive as Stewart's, or as the "Rules of Civility" set out by George Washington, the founding father of etiquette. Young George's sixth rule, for example, applies to reading this book: "Sleep not when others Speak."

General Rules of Proper Behavior

1. When you're at a seated dinner party, and you notice a cockroach climbing the wall, turn to your hostess and say brightly, "Oh my, Mrs. -------, but I do declare, you have an uninvited visitor!"

2. When deciding which fork to use with shrimp, remember: The shrimp doesn't care.

3. Never compare the physical appearance of an oyster to anything.

4. Don't even think about changing the color of your house unless you are on good terms with your neighbors, your neighborhood association and your municipal government.

5. When asking a neighbor for permission to use his narrow side yard in order to get access to the side of your house so it can be painted, remember first to return the soup tureen that belonged to his great-grandmother.

6. When you visit a Market-area bar and your shoes get stuck to the floor because it's coated with old beer, it is acceptable to go barefoot. The same applies when Market Street is flooded, that is to say, when it rains.

7. When addressing comments to an elected official during a public meeting and your opinion on the issue differs from that of the politician, it is unacceptable to refer to said politician as "Most Honorable Pointy-head."

8. In the misery of Lowcountry summer heat, short sleeves or no sleeves are proper clothing options, and you are permitted to amble.

9. As a host, you must keep the sheets clean and the door open for guests. You must also serve out-of-towners breakfast, lunch/dinner and supper, or meet them in restaurants for meals, tell them where to park, tell them what to see and do, and give them directions.

10. As a visitor, you are impolite to visit in July when it is hot or August when it is hotter and more miserable. If you must visit in August, do not ask your host to sit outside.

11. It is impolite to blow the car horn in anger or at stoplights.

12. If someone blows the horn at you, feel free to get out of your car, walk back to the offending driver's window and ask, "I beg your pardon. Did you summon me?"

13. It is impolite to correct tour guides, even when you hear one say, "This is the house where Rhett Butler used to sit naked on the porch of."

14. During high tea, it is permissible to pour a dash of alcohol into your cup so long as you are able to subsequently maintain a standard of behavior that does not damage the porcelain.

15. It is never proper to crash a ball, gala or other formal

party, even if you're dressed like Elvis.

16. Golf balls hit to alligators are out of bounds and may not be retrieved.

17. Roasted peanuts are for squirrels. Peanuts must be boiled in brine at home or bought from Tony the Peanut Man or another proper outlet.

18. All rules of proper behavior and expression are off whenever a dislocated pluffmudder is forced to drive in the snow.

19. On all occasions where you are the guest, you must say: "I had a wonderful time!" "Oh, that was grilled rabbit? I loved it!" whether those things are true or not.

20. On all occasions where you are the host, you must say: "It was no trouble at all!" and, "Your children are so delightful!" or perhaps, "Your children are so energetic!"

21. When it's absolutely necessary to say something rude behind someone's back, you must say it *sotto voce* and follow it with "bless his heart," "bless her heart" or, in the case of large groups of people from *Off,* "bless their hearts."

22. In all situations in which you are caught firing a shotgun at squirrels in your neighbor's yard, you must not pretend it wasn't you. Acceptable responses are: "I thought it was New Year's Eve" or, "I thought I saw a panda."

23. On occasions in which you are pulled over by the police, you must 1) smile; 2) wait patiently; 3) make eye contact; and 4) accept blame for hitting the cow. You hit it. You can't deny it.

24. It is polite, and often wise, to make a reservation at your favorite restaurant instead of simply sauntering in and exclaiming, "Where the hell did all these people come from?"

25. If you're virtuous enough to attend church on Sun-

day morning, you can pretty much feel free to park anywhere you want except in the burial ground.

Also:

Say hello to people on the street. Order the seafood. You can eat some of it with your hands. Don't pull the Spanish moss off the trees. Don't eat the oleanders; they're poisonous. Don't feed the alligators — for obvious reasons. Don't go naked at the beach; again, for obvious reasons. Don't feed the laughing gulls; they're nasty. Three martinis might be too many, but maybe not. Do not step on palmetto bugs on the sidewalks; they're slippery when squished. Watch out for horses in the street; they're working. Watch out for college students in the alleys; they're passed out. Pedestrians have the right-of-way; except for horses.

Chapter 8

It's Not The King's English

The King's was not the only language the Lowcountry used to *parlez*. Germans, Dutch, Irish and French all settled here. West African slaves added words like yam, okra, tote, goober (peanut), benne, gumbo, biddy and kuda (turtle) as they developed the vocabulary, syntax and pronunciations of Gullah. As a result of this mix of nationalities and languages, Lowcountry folks are peculiar about pronunciation. They take great offense and remark on it if, for example, the local newscaster says "Cooper" like "Roofer" instead of the correct "Cooper" like "Looker" or, more accurate to native speech, "Cuppah."

This enthusiasm about pronunciation extends to historical research on the etymology of some unique terms. Like "piazza," which locals call their big porches and pronounce to rhyme with "axe," not "father." Robert Stockton, who teaches architecture and history at the College of Charleston, says: "Some fools have confused this perfectly good English word with the Italian word, pronounced 'pee-AT-za,' which means 'open square' and not 'porch.' We need a workshop to teach the proper pronunciation of this and other Lowcountry words."

A good understanding of French helps, thanks to the large influence Huguenots (French Protestants) have had on our culture in the last 400 years.

A few local French family names with proper pronunciation:

Legare: Luh-gree
Beaufain: Bew-fayne
Beaufort: Bew-fort. The city of the same name in the Carolina to the North: Bo-fort.
Huger: Yew-gee
Manigault: Mani-go
Prioleau: Pray-low
Horry: Oar-ee
Desaussure: Dess-a-soor
DeBordieu: Debby-do
Montagu: Mont-a-gew
Huguenot: Hue-guh-not
Gaillard: Gill-yard

A few English, Dutch, American Indian etc. names:

Cooper: Cuppah
Vanderhorst: Van-drawst
Kiawah: Kee-uh-waaah
Wadmalaw: Wawd-muh-law
Edisto: Ed-is-toe
Combahee: Cumby
Ashepoo: Ashy-poo
Yeamans: Yay-mans
Hasell: Hazel
Coosawhatchie: Coo-saw-hatchy

The Citadel: Cid-a-dull; Cit-a-dell only in football
   cheers that rhyme with hell.

A few translations from what you say to what we say:

Hair salon: Beauty parlor
Washer: Washin' machine
Yard: Garden
Barefoot: Barefooted
Grits: Hom'ny
Pilau, pilaf: Purr-low
Pharmacy: Drug sto'
Supermarket: Groshry sto'
Gnats: No-See-Ums
Lost an opportunity: Missed the boat
Winter weather: Cold as a cucumber
Summer weather: Hot as the hinges
In trouble: Up da crick
Refrigerator: Ice box
Purse: Pocketbook
Newcomer: Cum'yuh
Oldtimer: Bin'yuh
Originating elsewhere: From Off
Service station: Fullin' station
Early afternoon meal: Dunnah
Dinner: Suppah
Pillow: Pulla'
Dawn: Crackuhdawn, Crackuhday, Day Bust,
   Day Clean (after the sun is all the way up)
I'm leaving: I gwine

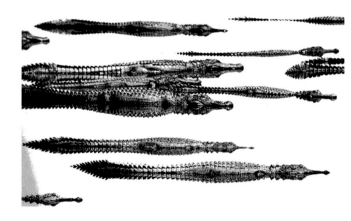

Chapter 9

Don't Feed the Alligators, etc.

The Lowcountry view takes in the food chain in all its gory splendor: a great blue heron eating a black snake, an eagle eating a marsh rat, a red-tailed hawk eating a mockingbird. These predators aren't just rural. Suburbanites are sometimes shocked to find alligators in the back yard, a water moccasin on the kitchen floor, raccoons in the attic and a possum in the washing machine.

Some residents like to play a game called "Scare the Visitors." They think it's real funny to tell their guests that an alligator looks upon their cute little poodle as a delicious snack cracker, or that the palmetto bugs can fly. A Berkeley County lawyer, for example, says he had to excuse himself from the dinner table to deal with an alligator that was outside scaring his horses. His dinner guests were from Iowa.

Like all good stories, those about animals can veer wildly away from the truth, but are told as absolute fact. A Sullivan's Islander relates the story of a friend with a shrimp farm on Edisto Island. Into the shrimp enclosure climbed a blue crab that stayed in one spot and gorged himself on shrimp, using alternate claws. The happy crab grew so fat that he measured 13 inches from shell point to shell point, or so the story goes.

For those who want to get to know frogs better (we don't know who that might be), a James Island wildlife biologist recommends Frogwatch USA, which has recordings of the croaks, squawks, blats and tremors of every type of frog in the state. Voices in the spring and summer Tree Frog Chorus include Southern leopard frogs, barking tree frogs, bird-voiced tree frogs, ornate chorus frogs, pig frogs, Southern chorus frogs (from which the Tree Frog Chorus takes its name) and spring peepers. Members of the Greater Frog Symphony Orchestra include the American toad, the Eastern narrow-mouth toad and the booming bass of the American bullfrog, among others.

But enough about frogs. Other wildlife gets our attention, too.

Palmetto bugs: What most people call cockroaches, we politely refer to as palmetto bugs. They can be up to three inches long and they do fly. They use the city sidewalks freely. Leave your car window open and you're likely to have one riding shotgun.

Mosquitoes: Mosquitoes like some individuals better than others. No, really. The little bloodsuckers, to put it politely, have receptors that home in on people giving off the most carbon dioxide and other chemicals — what scientists call "a good quality blood meal." Wear DEET or flail about in constant motion outdoors. If all you have is a citronella candle but no matches, simply slather the wax all over you like soap.

No-see-ums: These are gnats, known as "flying teeth."

They take sustenance from gnawing on your ears, your face, and your scalp by the thousands. Look at one under a microscope; it's all mouth. Bug spray deters them not at all, and Skin So Soft makes them hungrier. But Lowcountry creek fishermen say WD-40 oil, which they normally use on reels, works as a short-term deterrent.

Shrimp: If you swim in creeks, you can sometimes feel them hitting your legs as they move out into the ocean from the estuaries where they were spawned.

Loggerhead turtles (*Caretta caretta*): These large sea turtles lay eggs in the sand in June and July and hatch in August and September. Volunteers on Lowcountry beaches locate nests, build protective hatcheries, relocate nests threatened by high tide or erosion, cage the nests for protection from predators, monitor and inventory them, and husband the hatchlings into the sea. Because hatchlings are drawn to light, the Lowcountry practices lights-out at night near the beaches during turtle season so they won't go the wrong way.

Snakes: Mr. No Shoulders, collectively speaking, is a longtime resident of the swamp. Mr. Copperhead, Mr. Cottonmouth and Mr. Canebrake Rattler are venomous and are not welcome, but a king snake and a rat snake in the crawl space or attic of your home means no mice, ever. However, who cares about mice if you're having a heart attack!

Wood ducks: Elegant, painterly little wood ducks, or summer ducks as we call them, live and nest year-round in hollow trees or in wooden manmade houses built specifically for them. If you live on, in or near a fresh-water swamp — which is just about anywhere in the Lowcountry — get in touch with the S.C. Department of Natural

Resources for instructions on how to build a nesting box for our prettiest resident duck.

Alligators (*Alligator mississippiensis)*: Their reptilian brains are about the size of a walnut, their teeth are as sharp as skinning knives, and their hides are as tough as a steel-belted tire. Yet they are generally shy of humans. But don't swim where large alligators swim and don't attempt to feed them. They have been known not only to bite the hand that offers them a snack but also take off an entire arm in the process. It's illegal to feed, harass or attempt to catch an alligator without a special state permit. A fed alligator becomes a nuisance gator, and a nuisance gator is put under a death sentence, says Walt Rhodes of the S.C. Department of Natural Resources.

Hummingbirds: The Lowcountry's most hyperactive bird is the only one that can hover and fly backward. They just love sugar water, but artificial sweeteners are deadly.

Bluebottle flies: Appropriately named *Calliphora vomitoria*, this big metallic-colored bug feasts on nectar, rotting fruit and, in the larval state, the decomposing flesh of dead animals.

Great blue herons: The marauder of the marsh is very territorial. Their appetites and stances, at nearly four feet high with a wingspan up to six feet, are gargantuan.

Chiggers: Also known as a "red bug," a chigger is a mite smaller than a period mark in the arachnid family, the same cozy group as scorpions and spiders. Chigger bites welt up and itch for weeks. If you have been out in the woods, then come home and find that you are covered in redbug bites, ignore a local's advice that you should submerge yourself in a tub full of Clorox. This does not work and it's bad for your skin. The favorite Lowcountry antidote is a dab of fingernail polish — any color will do — placed directly onto the welt. This apparently covers the itty-bitty puncture wound and blocks out air for up to six hours, if you're lucky. The itch typically resumes while the victim is asleep or standing on a ladder changing a light bulb.

NOTE: Dead trees — which we call "snags" — are not useless eyesores. They're vital to wildlife habitat. Many of our friendly little neighbors live in snags; they offer up a feast of nutritious insects for woodpeckers and others. Wood ducks build nests in woodpecker holes carved out of dead trees, and they preen while sitting on low-hanging branches. Lots of wading and diving birds perch on snags. These include numerous kinds of herons and egrets, ibis and other wood storks, as well as anhinga, those large "snake birds" that dive into freshwater ponds and slither along the bottom in search of small fish and other seafood, then surface, claw their way back up to their perch and spread their wings to dry. Anhinga have no oil in their feathers, which allows them to stay under water for long periods of time, but makes their bodies waterlogged once they get back out. Therefore, they sit and spread their wings for a while to let air and sun do the job.

Chapter 10

Myths, Superstitions and Outright Lies

A mong the snow beasts, haunted houses, alien sightings and ghost stories in the book "Weird U.S.: Your Travel Guide to America's Local Legends and Best Kept Secrets" are the Pawley's Island Gray Man, who walks the beach before a hurricane, and the Ravenel Lights, which appear on the road after you knock three times on a certain Baptist church door in that little town. This is a pitiful representation of the ghosts and eccentricities of the Lowcountry, which has some of the oldest ghosts and eccentricities in America. Okay, ghosts don't age, but you see the point. Ours are *historic*.

Myths can include explanatory stories, legendary doings, pervasive misreading or revision of historical fact, and the fame, or infamy, of one's ancestors. Southerners tend to stretch the truth about their ancestors as part of the region's endemic ancestor worship. Three more things that are regularly exaggerated around here are the age of live oaks, the size of alligators and the severity of the weather.

Grand trees in the Lowcountry are those with trunks at least 24 inches in diameter at a point 4½ feet from the ground. One of the grandest — Angel Oak, just off Bohicket Road on Johns Island — is about 65 feet tall. Its trunk is 25½ feet in circumference, or 8½ feet in diameter measured 4½ feet off the ground. Its canopy shades more than 17,000 square feet. Its biggest limb has a circumference of 11½ feet and is 89 feet long.

The property around Angel Oak was granted to Abraham Waight in 1717 and the tree got its name when descendant Martha Waight married Justis Angel in 1810. Angel Oak is routinely said to be 1,400 years old, but Charleston's urban forester Danny Burbage estimates it's 500 years old at the most. The exact age of large oaks is difficult to determine, even when the tree is dead, because of heart rot, Burbage says. Also, their wide trunks often consist of the merged trunks of several trees.

According to the School of Forest Resources at the University of Georgia:

"The largest (live oak) trees which remain in most of the native range, especially along the Atlantic coast, are seldom over 200 years old, with a maximum expected lifespan of 400 years. Many old, large trees have myths develop around them regarding their age and historic value. Many large live oaks are not as old as people believe."

That doesn't mean that *Quercus virginiana*, the Southern live oak, is not special. Enslaved Africans and their Gullah descendants believed that spirits lived in these and other Lowcounty trees. Indeed, if the time is right and you listen very carefully, you can hear them whispering.

As for that alligator in your back yard, he is not 20 feet long. The largest *Alligator mississippiensis* on record in the United States measured 19 feet 2 inches. It was trapped in Louisiana in the early 1900s. Today, according to the

S.C. Department of Natural Resources, male alligators can reach 13 feet.

Now for the weather. The word "hurricane" comes from Huracan, the name of the Mayan god of wind and Carib Indian god of evil. Since Hurricane Hugo raked the Lowcountry in 1989, we don't like to mention the H word, and we approach hurricane season with more than a little trepidation. We sometimes find ourselves cowering in the bathtub with a sofa cushion over our heads when the weatherman announces "golf ball-size hail" and an "approaching tornado," or notes in a grim voice that Tropical Depression 7 is on the way to the South Carolina coast before it's cleared the Cape Verde Islands. That's not to say the Lowcountry doesn't have severe thunderstorms, the odd tornado and the occasional H word.

Your humble author makes a particular cookie — pecan, caramel, chocolate-chunk, with a secret ingredient that is a powerful talisman against tropical storms. They've worked 10 times out of 11; on the 11th, the baker was out of town.

Moving on, we note two unusual 19th-century occasions that, contrary to the title of this chapter, actually happened.

Leviathan

Among Charleston's notable oddities is the whale skeleton that hangs overhead in The Charleston Museum on Meeting Street. These are the bones of a right whale that made the fatal mistake of wandering into Charleston Harbor in 1880. It was chased and killed by means of gigs, poles, guns and being run over repeatedly by boats, and hauled to a downtown wharf, where it was hung by its tail and its oil was rendered while on display to the gawking public at a small fee. When the carcass began to ripen, it was hauled across the Cooper River to shallow water and left for the crabs. Museum curator Gabriel Manigault later flensed the bones and articulated the skeleton for display at the museum, which was housed at The College of Charleston.

The January 1880 News and Courier account went on for pages of grandiose, excitable prose:

"Steamers, Tugs and Row Boats Join the Chase, which Lasts All Day — Desperate Efforts of the Monster to Escape — He Leads his Pursuers Backwards and Forwards Across the Harbor — The Death at Sunset — Fifty Feet Long and Fifteen Feet Thick.

"Several days ago the almost unprecedented presence of a whale in Charleston Harbor was announced. How he came hither, to a place so remote from his usual haunts, and so isolated from his friends and relations must forever remain a mystery. Whether driven here by stress of weather, seeking misanthropic seclusion from his kind or on an exploring expedition will never be known, but his presence was a huge, black verity." A 1905 bulletin of the college museum notes in a list of exhibits the "Black Whale, Norcaper, or Biscay Whale, *Baleana Glacialis Bonnaterre*: This is the skeleton of a young male captured in Charleston Harbor Jan. 8, 1880, and mounted by Dr. Gabriel E. Manigault, then Curator of the Museum. The length of this animal in the flesh was 40 feet 4 inches. The skeleton measures 35 feet 7 inches. Fortunately, the greater part of the baleen plates or 'whalebone' is shown in its natural position in the jaws."

Memorial Day

Memorial Day has taken on the solemn task of paying tribute to victims of foreign wars. But the modern observance of Memorial Day has domestic roots. It began with grieving American citizens mourning the losses of Union and Confederate troops.

Charleston can claim the first Memorial Day. David W. Blight, author of "Race and Reunion: The Civil War in American Memory," describes the May 1, 1865, occasion, called Decoration Day, at what is now Hampton Park:

"After Charleston, South Carolina, was evacuated in February 1865 near the end of the Civil War, most of the people remaining among the ruins of the city were thousands of blacks. During the final eight months of the war, Charleston had been bombarded by Union batteries and gunboats, and much of its magnificent architecture lay in ruin. Also during the final months of war, the Confederates had converted the Planters' Race Course (a horse track) into a prison in which some 257 Union soldiers had died and were thrown into a mass grave behind the grandstand.

"In April, more than 20 black carpenters and laborers went to the grave site, reinterred the bodies in proper graves, built a tall fence around the cemetery enclosure 100 yards long and built an archway over an entrance. On the archway, they inscribed the words, 'Martyrs of the Race Course.' And with great organization on May 1, 1865, the black folk of Charleston, in cooperation with white missionaries, teachers and Union troops, conducted an extraordinary parade of approximately 10,000 people.

"It began with 3,000 black schoolchildren marching around the Planters' Race Course with armloads of roses and singing 'John Brown's Body.' Then followed the black women of Charleston and then the men. They were in turn followed by members of Union regiments and various white abolitionists such as James Redpath. The crowd gathered in the graveyard; five black preachers read from Scripture; and a black children's choir sang 'America,' 'We Rally Around the Flag,' the 'Star-Spangled Banner' and several spirituals. Then the solemn occasion broke up into an afternoon of speeches, picnics and drilling troops on the infield of the old planters' horseracing track.

"This was the first Memorial Day. Black Charlestonians had given birth to an American tradition. By their labor, their words, their songs, and their solemn parade of roses and lilacs and marching feet on their former masters' race course, they had created the Independence Day of the Second American Revolution."

Afterword

A Shot of Lagniappe for the Road

A monk was anxious to learn Zen and said to the Master: "I have been newly initiated into the brotherhood. Will you be gracious enough to show me the way to Zen?"

The Master said: "Do you hear the murmuring sound of the mountain stream? Here is the entrance."

Fellow students of the Lowcountry, do you hear the lapping of the waves on the shore? Is there a mackerel sky? Do you see the shadow of the live oak, the dull glint of winter light and the cold breath of the singing bird? Here is the entrance. Let the foghorns of ships in the harbor channel be your chimes, and take these Lowcountry received truths as mantras:

Consider the pelican. His bill can hold more than his belly can.

A new broom sweeps too hard.

The old broom knows the corners.

Every Lowcountry sky is a gift.

The glass is half-full.

Time and tide wait for no one.

Get your head out of the boat and onto the course.

It's not a good idea to stand with one foot on the boat
  and the other foot on the dock.
They call that thing "the boom" for a reason.
Old age is not for sissies.
Don't let the sugar settle into the bottom of the glass.
Go to the party. You'll have fun once you get there.
If you eat standing up, it doesn't count.
Drink the first martini, sip the second, sniff the third.
Nothing exceeds like excess.
Work is not fun. That's why they call it work.
Things take longer than you think they will.
Remember to do nothing when nothing is required.
Any time you get a chance, take a nap.
The point of fishing is not to catch fish.
Laissez les bon temps rouler! (Let the good times roll!)
Plus ça change, plus c'est la même chose. (The more things
  change, the more they stay the same.)
The Lowcountry has four seasons — Almost Summer,
  Summer, Still Summer and Hanukkah/Christmas.
It can't be this hot and not rain.
Wait for the cool spell in August.
It sometimes arrives in October.
The best journey is the road home.

— The End —